Celts for Kids

An Enthralling Overview of Celtic History, Ancient Britons, and Their Conflicts with the Romans

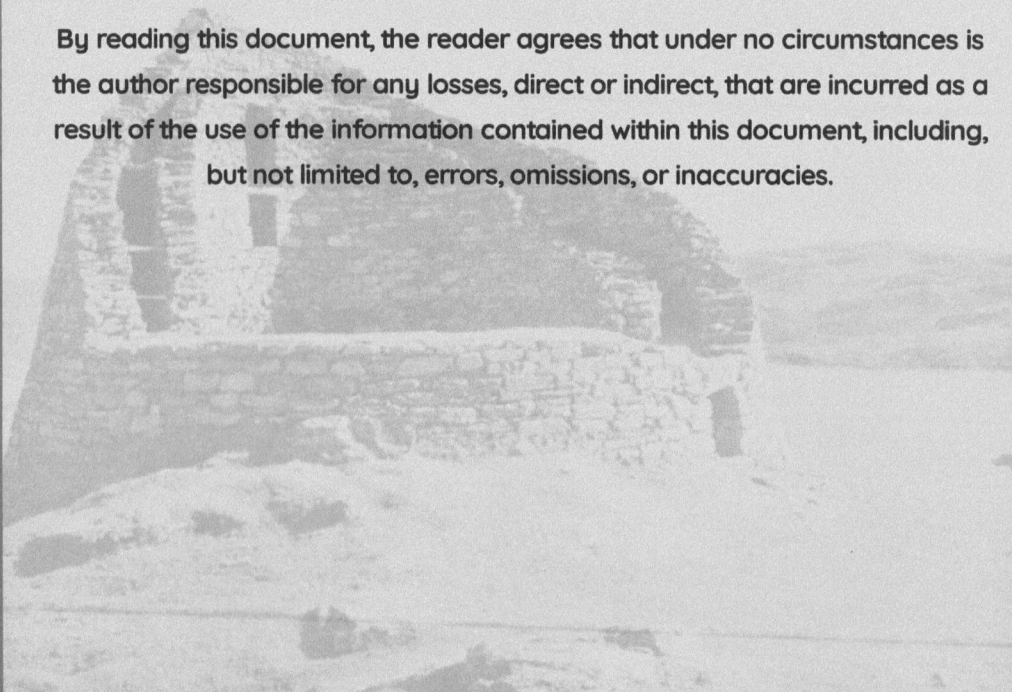

Table of Contents

INTRODUCTION

Have you ever heard of genealogy, the science of genetics, and DNA? DNA is like a fingerprint of our bodies. It is carried in every cell. Every person has a unique mix of DNA. Scientists who research people's origins and their descendants can use DNA to trace human ancestry, the places where they lived, and much more. These scientists are called geneticists.

Genetic science has become one of the most valuable tools for tracing ancient and modern people's heritage. That is why we know so much more about the Celts than people did just a few decades ago.

Much of what we know about the Celts comes from piecing together art and artifacts (objects) excavated by archaeologists because the Celts did not leave written records. Grave goods (items buried with the dead) are particularly valuable in figuring out what people used and treasured.

The written records we have about the ancient Celts were written by their enemies, the Greeks and Romans. The Celts' history and folklore were only written down during the Middle Ages. Their history was intertwined with legends and myths of magic, invincible heroes, and supernatural beings.

Are you ready to explore who the Celts are, where they came from, how they lived, and where and who they are today? Then, let's get started!

There were many Celtic tribes. During a period we call the Iron Age, groups or tribes who shared a similar language and similar habits lived all over the middle and western parts of Europe. These tribes became known collectively as the Celts.

The Celts were not a united nation. Celts married outside their tribes. They also brought other people and ethnic groups into their tribes. They picked up habits and borrowed words from several other cultures as they mixed and spread across Europe.

Captivating Facts

- The Celts did not call themselves Celts. Each tribe had its own name.
- The terms Celtic and Gaelic were first used as recently as the 1700s CE in Old English writing.

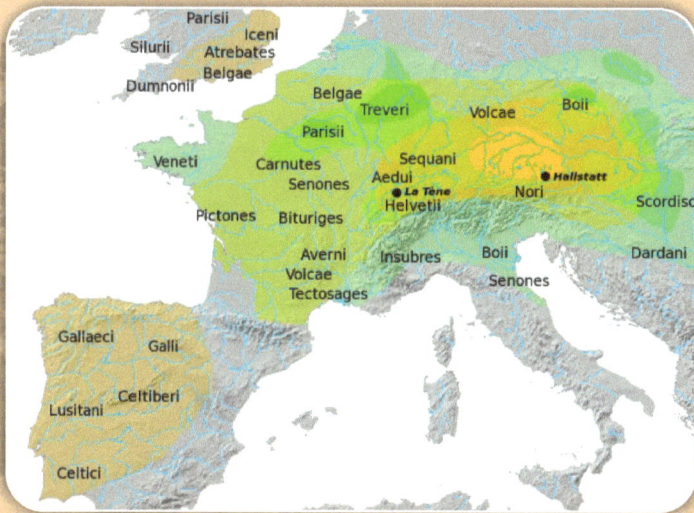

Spreading of Celtic tribes in the Iron Age.

- The Celts did not come from one place, and they did not all end up in the same place.
- For ages, scholars believed the Celts originated with the Hallstatt culture in Austria and became the La Téne culture in Switzerland. Now, they are not so sure because similar artifacts from the same time were found in other places!

The Iron Age

The Iron Age is the name that scholars give to a time in history when humans learned to use iron. Before that, people were using bronze, which is a metal made from copper melted together with a bit of tin. This was known as the Bronze Age. The period before that was known as the Stone Age because people made tools and objects from stone and wood.

Model of the Hallstatt settlement.

Neitram – Edited version of this photo: File: Archäologisches Museum Königsbrunn Modell Hallstattzeitliche Siedlung 01.jpg, CC BY-SA 4.0, https://commons.wikimedia.org/w/index.php?curid=117205740

Celtic Roots

We do not know for sure where the Celts came from. Scientists and scholars even argue about when the Celtic culture started. Remnants of their daily life have been traced back more than three thousand years to around 1200 BCE in parts of Europe.

Their culture was first identified around the Hallstatt settlements in Austria. They thrived off their valuable salt mines. Salt was an essential commodity for all ancient peoples. They didn't have refrigerators or preservatives to keep food fresh! But ancient people were innovators. They used salt to preserve and dry their food to keep it from rotting.

Their trail is later picked up again at La Téne in Switzerland around 450 BCE. It was the same culture, although their metalworking and daily lives were more advanced than the Hallstatt culture.

Around this same time, some Celtic tribes migrated to Britain and Ireland. Groups of Celts had already settled there. They had mixed with the local inhabitants.

The Name "Celts"

Some early Celtic tribes in mainland Europe moved south across the Alps to today's Switzerland and France. They met the Greeks. The Greeks had a trading port on the Mediterranean Sea at Massalia (today's Marseille in France). The Celts were given the name "Keltoi," meaning foreigners or barbarians, by ancient Greek writers in 517 BCE.

Celts migrated farther westward and southward over time. By around 500 BCE, Celts had already settled in parts of Spain and France and spread to Britain and Ireland.

The Celts eventually settled in four main areas:

- Tribes that settled in most of today's France, Italy, Belgium, and Switzerland were called the Gauls by the Romans. The Romans conquered them in the Gallic Wars. These Cults adopted the Roman culture.

- The tribes who settled in England, Scotland, and Wales were called the Britons. The term Britons includes the pre-Celtic inhabitants as well.

- The third main group of tribes lived on the Isle of Man (Mannin in Gaelic) and in Ireland (Eire *(eye-ree)* in Irish or Gaelic). They were known as the Gaels. The Gaelic language dialects are called Goidelic *(goy-del-ik)*. The Gaels later lived in Scotland (Alba in Gaelic).

Celtic huts in Galicia, Spain.

- The fourth group settled in the northwest of Spain in an area called Galicia. They were called Gallaeci *(Ga-lee-see)*. Their descendants still live there, and they speak a Celtic language. They also celebrate Celtic pagan festivals.

Some scholars believe that the migration of the Celts to Britain and Ireland happened slowly over many years. Others are convinced that the main branches moved in mass *(large)* migrations. During a migration, people move with everything they own to settle in new lands.

Remember the study of genetics that we talked about earlier? Well, geneticists tested the DNA of large groups of modern-day people in the United Kingdom and Ireland. They compared the DNA to ancient Celtic DNA. They concluded that the Celts moved there in several migrations, both large and small, over time.

Although this seems complex, it is very exciting for geneticists, linguists, anthropologists, archaeologists, and historians. It is like a gigantic puzzle they have to work together on to discover the roots of the Celts and other ancient peoples. Maybe the most interesting discovery so far this century is that the ancient Celts did not have a single genetic origin or ethnic identity.

Chapter 1 Activity

Can you tell which of the following is true or false?

	Question	True	False
1.	The Celts came from China.		
2.	Celts spread to England during the Stone Age.		
3.	Celts learned to do carpentry (woodwork) in the Iron Age.		
4.	Celts were ruthless invaders of new countries.		
5.	Celts were masters of iron crafts.		
6.	Celtic culture can be traced back to Hallstatt in Austria.		
7.	Celts still live in Galicia, Spain, with their own habits, language, and festivals.		
8.	The Celts mixed with other ethnic and tribal groups.		
9.	Historians know all about the Celts from reading their books.		
10.	Other people lived in Britain before the Celts arrived.		

Chapter 1 Answers

	Question	True	False
1.	The Celts came from China.		✗
2.	Celts spread to England during the Stone Age.		✗
3.	Celts learned to do carpentry (woodwork) in the Iron Age.		✗
4.	Celts were ruthless invaders of new countries.		✗
5.	Celts were masters of iron crafts.	✗	
6.	Celtic culture can be traced back to Hallstatt in Austria.	✗	
7.	Celts still live in Galicia, Spain, with their own habits, language, and festivals.	✗	
8.	The Celts mixed with other ethnic and tribal groups.	✗	
9.	Historians know all about the Celts from reading their books.		✗
10.	Other people lived in Britain before the Celts arrived.	✗	

Today, most of the Celtic culture is linked to Ireland, Scotland, Wales, the Isle of Man, Galicia (a tip of Spain), and Brittany (the tip of France).

Ireland already had inhabitants when the Celts arrived. In recent years, geneticists discovered some ancient people in Ireland had Middle Eastern DNA. They had dark skin, black hair, and brown eyes. Later people, Celts included, brought genes with more diversity (differences) in skin, hair, and eye colors. The most ancient DNA so far analyzed in Britain belonged to a young man with a very dark complexion, black hair, and bright blue eyes.

Tombs, Cairns, and Mounds

There are world-famous burial sites and cairns (stacked rocks that can serve as burial monuments) in Ireland that date back thousands of years before the Iron Age and final Celtic migrations. We do not know who these builders were, but some of their monuments were intricately built.

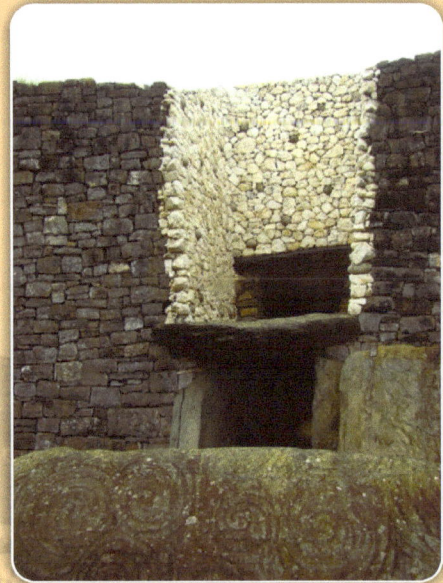

The entrance to Newgrange.
Sharon Drummond; https://creativecommons.org/licenses/by/2.0/. https://flickr.com/photos/28085418@N07/4353267409

The Celts made use of these sites, although we cannot be sure for what exact purposes. The mounds (hill-like soil and stone coverings of burials and ancient ruins) are surrounded by large stones with Celtic swirling designs carved into them.

Newgrange is one of the most famous sites in Ireland. Celtic patterns decorate the stones at the entrance to Newgrange.

At Newgrange, the ancient builders built a long passage ending in a burial chamber. They built the tomb so that the sun shines through a hole just above the entrance at dawn for six days around the winter solstice. The sunlight creeps down the passage as the sun rises until it reaches the back wall of the central burial chamber. Then, it lights up every corner of that pitch-dark room! How cool is that?

Newgrange and other great tombs are older than Stonehenge. They are also older than the famous pyramids of Egypt. They were built during the Stone Age. This shows us that the people who lived in Ireland before the Iron Age Celts arrived were advanced and had knowledge of mathematics and astronomy.

The Celts who moved to Ireland around 500 BCE mixed with these people groups. So, we can assume that they learned skills and knowledge from each other. They likely lived and worked together in communities. We can also assume that the newer Celts were the larger majority and absorbed the people already living in Ireland.

Quick Facts About Ireland

- **Ireland is called Eire in Gaelic.** Ireland is also known as the Emerald Isle because it is so lush and green.
- **Today, Ireland is bilingual.** They speak English and Irish Gaelic.

- **The national anthem of Ireland was influenced by the Celts.** "The Soldier's Song," or "Amrán na bhFiann" *(oh-rawn-na-vee-on)* in Irish, echoes the warrior traditions of the ancient Celts.

- **Saint Patrick's Day celebrates a major event in Ireland.** Saint Patrick was the Roman Catholic bishop who succeeded in converting the Irish Celts from paganism to Christianity. He cleverly incorporated *(combined)* ancient pagan traditions with Christian practices. The sacred pagan beliefs of the Celts were not threatened, and he could slowly make them relate to Christianity.

- **The Corlea Trackway was built over two thousand years ago.** This is an oak-planked road called a togher *(toe-ker)* in Irish that dates to 148 BCE. It was preserved in the peat bogs of Ireland. Archaeologists believe the Celts had wooden roads linking their trade settlements across Ireland and Britain.

- **The ancient Celts lived in roundhouses with thatched roofs.** Sometimes, they used stone for the walls. Other times, they used wattle and daub. The wattle-and-daub method involves weaving a structure with crisscrossed branches and covering it with clay. The clay was often mixed with dung. It was completely waterproof. The wattle-and-daub method was used all over the world by ancient cultures. It is still used today in some places!

- **High kings once ruled Ireland.** Celtic tribes in Ireland each had their own chieftains. Chieftains later became kings. Eventually, Ireland had a high king who was above all the other kings. These kings were crowned on the Hill of Tara, which is still seen as a sacred place in Ireland today.

- **Celtic tribes didn't always get along.** Celtic tribes were fiercely independent. However, they came together to fight off common enemies. They also fought regularly against each other.

- **In Ireland, Celtic women pretty much had the same rights as men.** Irish women were warriors, farmers, queens, and owners of property. They fought, worked, and ruled alongside men.

- **Celts practiced paganism.** Before Saint Patrick converted the Celts of Ireland to the Christian faith, they worshiped many gods. This is called polytheism. The gods of the Irish—and other Celts—were often connected to nature.

Druids telling the Britons to oppose the Roman landing.

- ▶ **Druids were very important in Celtic society.** They made the laws and taught people the rules of society. Druids were also priests, prophets, astronomers, poets, historians, and a lot more. Even the chiefs and kings listened to them!

- ▶ **Scholars are not sure when the Irish legal system was first introduced.** Brehon law was orally passed down from generation to generation via the Druids. It was only written down around 600 CE. Scholars think the basic laws were practiced by the earliest Celtic inhabitants of Ireland. The jurists were from the fili (*fee-lee*, a Gaelic word). They were the prophets, seers, poets, and historians of the Druids.

Another theory is that Brehon law and the Brehons *(keepers of the laws)* replaced the powerful Druids after Saint Patrick converted the people to Christianity. Brehon law ran without jails and police. Justice was based on restitution *(giving back)* as punishment.

Time for a word search! Can you find the words listed in the word bank?

E	M	E	R	A	L	D	L	M	N
P	C	L	O	V	E	R	A	O	E
A	H	E	H	F	B	U	Z	A	W
G	Y	P	A	T	R	I	C	K	G
A	C	G	R	B	E	D	F	X	R
N	L	O	P	T	D	S	K	V	A
P	Z	Y	R	B	R	E	H	O	N
V	S	W	T	L	M	K	U	I	G
R	D	M	G	A	E	I	L	G	E
J	V	N	O	Z	X	A	T	Q	P

Word Bank:

NEWGRANGE	OAK	BREHON
PATRICK	HARP	CLOVER
CORLEA	PAGAN	
EMERALD	DRUIDS	

E	M	E	R	A	L	D	L	M	N
P	C	L	O	V	E	R	A	O	E
A	H	E	H	F	B	U	Z	A	W
G	Y	P	A	T	R	I	C	K	G
A	C	G	R	B	E	D	F	X	R
N	L	O	P	T	D	S	K	V	A
P	Z	Y	R	B	R	E	H	O	N
V	S	W	T	L	M	K	U	I	G
R	D	M	G	A	E	I	L	G	E
J	V	N	O	Z	X	A	T	Q	P

Scientists from Oxford University performed widespread genetic tests a few years ago. They were surprised to discover that ancient Celtic DNA from the Isle of Man, Wales, Scotland, Ireland, and England significantly differed. This means that even though the Celts shared cultural and linguistic kinship *(family ties)*, they were not related to the same ancestors!

Scholars do not agree on who was already settled in Britain before the Celts arrived. We do know those ancient people built monuments like Stonehenge thousands of years before the Iron Age. They were probably descendants of earlier European migrants, including earlier Celts.

Wales

Welsh people are proud of their Celtic ancestry. Celtic names are found all over Wales in people and place names. The Welsh name for Wales is Cymru.

Celtic hut at the Museum of Welsh Life.
Nick Mutton; https://creativecommons.org/licenses/by-sa/2.0/. https://www.geograph.org.uk/photo/2003670

The people of Wales have the most DNA of the unknown ancient peoples who arrived after the end of the last ice age around twelve thousand years ago. Did they share common ancestry with the later Celts who migrated to Wales?

Hillfort Settlements

Celtic settlements often developed around hillforts. There are remains of over one thousand hillforts in Wales alone, but they are also spread all over Britain. Celts did not build hillforts only on hilltops. They built on level ground too. In some cases, more ditches and earthen or wooden banks were added for defense. Most dwellings were built inside the enclosures. Sometimes, even farm animals were kept inside.

Hillfort ruin in Britain.

https://commons.wikimedia.org/wiki/File:Aerial_photograph_of_Maiden_Castle,_1935.jpg

The chiefs and some of the elite lived in multistoried roundhouses.

Farmers sometimes lived outside the fortified settlement on the land where they planted their crops. Farmers planted wheat, barley, oats, rye, and hay. Farmers also kept cattle, pigs, horses, and sheep. Animals were often fed hay in the winter.

Celtic Tribes in Wales

Several Celtic tribes lived in Wales. The Silures *(si-li-ras)* lived in the valleys of southeast Wales. The Demetae *(de-me-ta -ee)* lived in southwestern Wales. The Ordovices *(or-do-visis)* settled in central and northwestern Wales. In the northeast, the Deceangli *(dec-ang-li)* were the dominant tribe.

Welsh and English are the official languages of Wales today. Welsh or Cymraeg *(come-raag)* developed from the Celtic language. In the 1500s CE, King Henry VIII made English the only official language in Britain. It was only in the last century that Welsh regained its official status.

Britain's Celts had writing, but they did not use it very often. Knowledge about mathematics, astronomy, medicine, history, and other subjects was preserved by the Druids. No written records from the Druids remain today.

Poets and singers called bards learned songs, stories, and poems by heart. They belonged to a class of Druids. They traveled from place to place, singing and reciting history and folk tales.

Cornwall

Iron Age life in Cornwall, a county in England, was much the same, with many hillforts and villages with roundhouses.

There were also houses with stables, granaries, and rooms opening onto a large courtyard.

The most fascinating Iron Age buildings in Cornwall are the *fogous (foo-goos)*. These were deep trenches or ditches in the ground covered with stone slabs for roofs. The sides were lined with large stone slabs.

Historians and archaeologists are still not sure what the purpose of these underground structures was. Some think they were mainly for food storage. Others think they were used as meeting places or as shelters during enemy attacks.

Inside a well-preserved fogou in Cornwall.

One of the dominant Celtic tribes that settled in Cornwall was the Dumnonii *(dum-no-ni-i)*. Recent genetic tests show that the people of Cornwall are from different Celtic origins than their close neighbors in Devon.

Tin was a very important resource. It was mined in the west of Cornwall. Tin was needed to make copper into bronze. Even after people learned how to smelt iron ore and use iron for their weapons and tools, bronze remained an important metal for household tools, art, and jewelry.

Scholars know Celtic merchants traded tin ingots *(blocks of metal)* from Cornwall with the Greek colony in Massalia (today's Marseille) and the Middle East because of shipwrecks on those trade routes.

Cornwall and its people are mentioned around 325 BCE by an ancient Greek writer named Pytheas. He came from Massalia. Pytheas described the people of Cornwall as civilized. His words were repeated later by Diodorus Siculus, a famous ancient Greek historian. That was a great compliment. The ancient Greeks often called other people groups barbarians and looked down on them.

Cornish Gaelic died out as a living language around 1800 CE, but it has been revived. It has even been officially recognized by the British government. Some signage, such as place names, have been added in Cornish. The language is also taught in several primary schools.

Scotland

When we think of Scotland, the first things that usually come to mind are kilts (the short checkered skirts worn by men), bagpipe music, and stories of the Loch Ness Monster.

Scotland was greatly influenced by the Celtic culture. When the Iron Age Celts arrived in Scotland, groups of people were already living there. The strongest tribe they met was the Picts, who lived in the north and northeast of Scotland.

The Picts might have been descendants of earlier Celtic migrants from northern Europe, but historians are not sure where they came from. They are believed to have had mostly red hair. They tattooed themselves and often painted their bodies.

Painting of Saint Columba converting the Picts to Christianity.
William Hole, CC BY-SA 3.0 <https://creativecommons.org/licenses/by-sa/3.0>,
via Wikimedia Commons; https://commons.wikimedia.org/wiki/File:Saint_Columba_converting_the_Picts.jpg

Genetic tests from this century show that 10 percent of today's men in Scotland are direct descendants of the red-headed Picts. This means the Picts were absorbed into the later Scottish tribes.

The Romans described the people in Scotland as wild, barbaric people who painted themselves with blue paint. However, the Romans might have been a little frustrated with the people in Scotland. The Romans never succeeded in conquering parts of today's Scotland for long. They were always stopped by a fierce alliance of tribes.

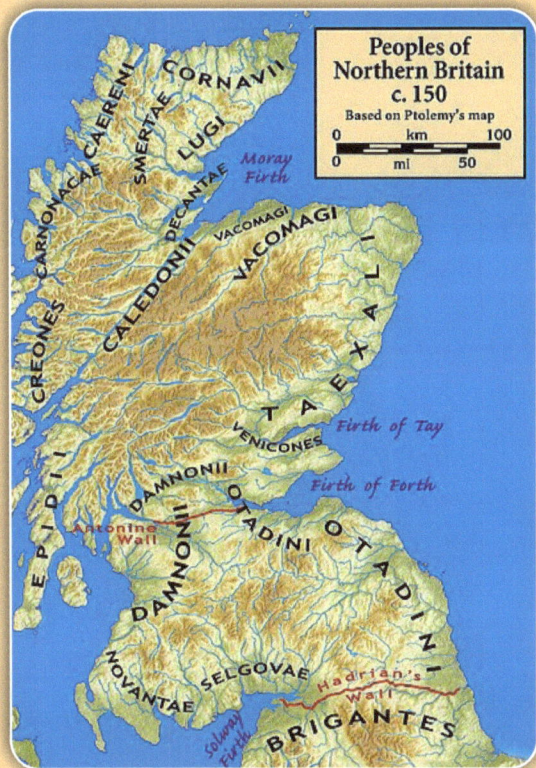

Celtic tribes in the north of Britain according to an ancient map by Ptolemy.

The Scottish tribes kept raiding the north of England whenever the Romans got a foothold. They were such a nuisance that Roman Emperor Hadrian began to build his famous wall in 122 CE to mark the border between his land and theirs!

England

Celtic tribes settled across most of England. At times, closely related tribes were taken over by their neighbors. For instance, we know from Julius Ceasar's writings that the Trinovantes *(try-no-van-tees)* and Cantiaci *(kan-tee-ya-cee)* tribes were taken over by their bigger neighbors, the Catuvellauni *(ka-tu-ve-lawny)*.

These tribes shared the same social habits and religion. They ate from plates and drank from cups. They cremated *(burned)* their dead.

The tribes in the southeast of England had ties with French and Mediterranean peoples. They followed some of the same customs. These connections date to the time of the Iron Age or even before.

There was much trade across the English Channel even before the Romans invaded. We know that some of the people from across the Channel fled to England when the Romans conquered their territories.

Iron Age Tribes south of Scotland according to Ptolemy's map.

One of the most wealthy and prosperous tribes that we know of was the Iceni *(ee-cee-ny)*. Some of the richest Iron Age finds of gold and bronze objects were from the areas where the Iceni dwelled.

The king of the Iceni did not object to Roman occupation. He became one of Rome's client kings and shared power with the Romans.

Trouble after his death led to the most successful Celtic revolt against Roman occupation. The Iceni, led by Queen Boudica *(boo-duh-kuh)*, and their tribal allies beat the Romans in several large battles. Eventually, the Iceni were defeated.

The Isle of Man

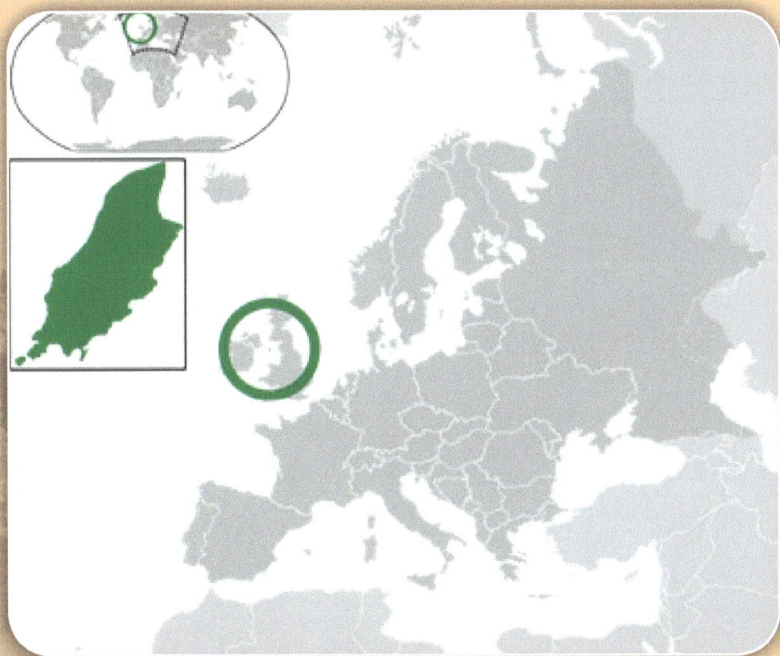

The Isle of Man is located in the middle of the Irish Sea between Britain and Ireland.

The people of the Isle of Man have a rich cultural Celtic background. One of their official languages, Manx, is a Celtic language. English is their other official language. The island is named after the Celtic sea god, Manannán. The Isle of Man is a self-ruling Crown Dependency of the United Kingdom.

The Isle of Man is close to Scotland. Traders and raiders targeted the island because of its position and its rich mineral resources. Even the Norse Vikings set up a thriving trade colony there around 820 CE. In 1266, the island was given to Scotland as part of a deal with the Norse king.

Can you figure out the answers to the crossword below?

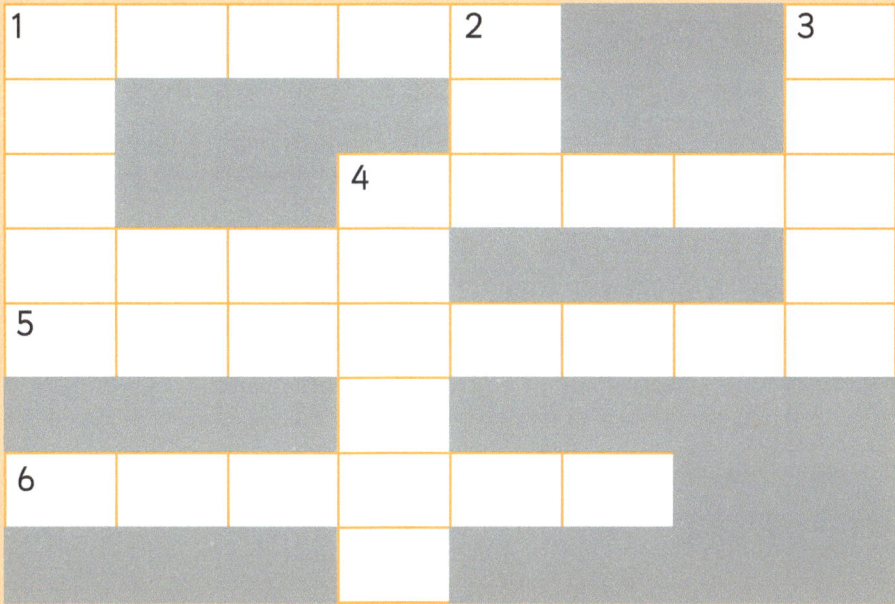

B	R	O	C	H				R
A				A				O
R			C	Y	M	R	U	
D			A				N	
S	C	O	T	L	A	N	D	
			T					
B	A	R	L	E	Y			
			E					

Dwellings

The Celts traditionally lived in hillforts (settlements built on higher ground). In these settlements, the chieftains lived at the top with their families. The soldiers lived on a lower level. The craftsmen and metalworkers lived below them. There were ditches, mounds of soil, or wooden fences around these hillforts. Villagers, farmers, and peasants sometimes lived outside these borders.

The Celts of Britain lived in roundhouses. These hut-like structures had just one room. It had a fireplace in the center and a built-in bread oven. It also had storage spaces around the sides and in the roof. A big pot called a cauldron hung over the fireplace. The cauldrons were usually made of bronze. Everything was cooked in it.

Largest of the replica Iron-Age roundhouses, Butser Farm.
ick Smith, CC BY-SA 2.0 <https://creativecommons.org/licenses/by-sa/2.0>,
via Wikimedia Commons;https://commons.wikimedia.org/w/index.php?curid=106409542

Other Structures

Celts sometimes built houses on a manufactured island in a loch *(lake)* for safety. This island was called a crannog *(kra-nog)*. Traces of crannogs can still be found in Wales, Scotland, and Ireland.

Wealthy families also lived in brochs. These were round, multistoried structures made of stone. They had steps on the inside around the outer walls. Many ruins of these structures can still be found in Scotland.

Ruins of Dun Carloway Broch in Scotland.
Bikerhiker75, CC BY-SA 4.0 <https://creativecommons.org/licenses/by-sa/4.0>,
via Wikimedia Commons; https://commons.wikimedia.org/wiki/File:Broch_Dun_Carloway_Lewis_Schottland.jpg

Fireplace and Firedog

The fireplace warmed the room when it was cold. It was used to cook things and to provide light. The smoke from the fire would spread into the thatched roof. The smoke acted like a natural deterrent for bugs and vermin. All that smoke also fire-proofed the thatch. The fireplace was protected by iron frames on two sides.

The fireplace frame was called a firedog even though it did not look like a dog at all! It was a metal object that marked the edges of the fireplace on two sides. It kept the coals in place.

A firedog from Capel Garmon, Wales.
National Museum Wales, CC BY-SA 3.0 <https://creativecommons.org/licenses/by-sa/3.0>,
via Wikimedia Commons; https://commons.wikimedia.org/wiki/File:Capel_Garmon_Firedog.jpg

Daily Life

An average day for a Celt was filled with chores. They looked after their animals, planted and harvested crops, cleaned their homes, and made tools and food.

The Celts were very clean people. They even discovered how to make soap. This apparently happened by accident. Very hot fat from a roasting animal fell into the ashes of a fire. This process separated an alkaline *(opposite of acidic)* substance now known as lye from the ashes. Lye is still used to make soap and cleaners today.

The Celts used wheat to make bread. They made porridge and cakes from oats. Barley was used to make beer.

They also picked mushrooms, berries, and nuts. They hunted boar and deer. Their farm animals were typically cattle, sheep, and pigs.

Celts also had horses if they were lucky enough to afford them. Some scholars believe the Celts viewed horses as sacred. Horses were a prized possession. The elite, warriors, and even farmers could be skilled riders and charioteers. Horses were mostly used for transporting goods, traveling, and in war. In the Shetland Islands, tail hairs from Shetland ponies were used to make fishing lines.

The Celts made their own utensils and tools. They were taught chores and skills like basket weaving, woodworking, and making clay pots from a young age. Skilled artists made jewelry for the elite. A trained blacksmith made weapons and other metal objects like firedogs and plows.

Class Distinctions

There were classes in Celtic culture. Anthropologists *(people who study people and their lifestyles)* do not always agree on how many or exactly what classes. Generally, it is accepted that the chiefs and, later, kings, their families, and other important people were at the top. They were the elite. The next class had the warriors and artisans. The ordinary people, like farmers, were next. Most Celts were farmers. The servants and slaves were at the bottom. The slaves were usually people captured in battles.

Clothing and Jewelry

Clothes were obviously different in certain areas and at different times. It was dependent on the weather and the raw materials (flax plants for linen, sheep for wool, and berries and bark for dyes) available in the area.

Women weaved wool and linen cloth on a loom. A loom is a frame on which threads are stretched tightly in one direction. Another thread is then woven across the stretched threads. This is continued, row after row, until you have a piece of cloth from which clothing can be made.

Celtic clothes were often colorful and patterned. Their tartan *(checkered)* clothes were the forerunners of the Scottish kilt. They also made clothes from leather and animal skins.

A pin brooch.
https://en.wikipedia.org/wiki/ File:Bronze_zoomorphic_penannular_brooch.jpg

Men wore loose pants and a shirt. Women wore skirts and loose blouses or long dresses. The Druids mostly wore long robes. Both men and women wore jewelry. The most important piece of jewelry was a pin brooch, which was used to pin their clothes together.

A loose cloak was used as a coat in cold weather. It was pulled together on the shoulder by a brooch or a pin. A brooch was also used to show the importance or wealth of a person.

Important people like chiefs and kings often wore metal neckbands. This was a beautifully decorated tight-fitting necklace called a torc. Most torcs had decorated open ends at the front. A torc could be made of bronze, silver, copper, or gold.

Ordinary people wore bracelets and necklaces made of leather, metal beads, or shells.

The Mysterious Druids

Druids were intellectuals and guardians of Celtic knowledge, history, and oral traditions. Poets and musicians from the Druid class, called bards, told folktales. They recited myths of heroes and ancestors during festivals.

During festivals, there was dancing and games for the children. Festivals were dedicated to the gods. It was hoped that the gods would bring good weather for planting, growing, and harvesting. Livestock were also blessed in the hopes they would be healthy and have many offspring.

The Druids were in charge of all religious practices. They were also in charge of making the laws and watching over the morals of each community. They carefully guarded their secrets and knowledge.

According to Cicero (a Roman author who lived from 106 to 43 BCE), Druids were scientists. They knew medicine, astronomy, and physics. In another account from Roman sources, the Druids would try to stop tribal battles by running between the fighting tribes to separate them.

The Romans wiped the Druids out, so we can never be sure how much of their knowledge was made up. There are scholars who believe they kept secret written records that were destroyed by the Romans and Christians to root out paganism.

Afterlife

The Celts believed in an afterlife. They sent the dead off to the next world with great feasts and fanfare so that they would be welcomed in the next life. These festivities were celebrated with a lot of food and beer. Beer and food were also buried with the wealthy so they could have a big party when they arrived in the afterlife.

When the Celts were still living in central Europe around 530 BCE, they buried an important leader. His burial mound was discovered in 1968. From this burial site, scholars learned that important Celts were buried with a wagon on four wheels. In this case, the bed of the wagon was made of bronze. The body was placed on a built-in bed in the chamber.

The chieftain was dressed in elaborate gold clothing and had a solid gold torc around his neck. Honey beer remnants *(leftovers)* were found in a large bronze cauldron surrounded by drinking vessels.

In later burials, the wealthy were buried together with two-wheeled chariots. Bodies were usually laid out on built-in beds.

Reconstructed grave of Hochdorf chieftain.
Marsupium photographyhttps://www.flickr.com/people/43405950@N07,
CC BY-SA 2.5 <https://creativecommons.org/licenses/by-sa/2.5>,
via Wikimedia Commons; https://commons.wikimedia.org/wiki/File:
Hochdorf_Chieftain%27s_Grave_reconstruction.jpg

Can you figure out the missing words in the following sentences?

1. Celtic roundhouses were made of wattle and _____ and had thatched _____.

2. Celts used a big pot called a _____ for cooking.

3. A _____ kept coals from the fire in the center of the house from spilling over into the room.

4. Settlements were built inside and around a _____ f _____.

5. Elites often lived in multistoried roundhouses called _____.

6. The tail hairs of _____ l _____ ponies were used to make fishing lines.

7. Celts loved to drink _____.

1. Celtic roundhouses were made of wattle and **DAUB** and had thatched **ROOFS**.

2. Celts used a big pot called a **CAULDRON** for cooking.

3. A **FIREDOG** kept coals from the fire in the center of the house from spilling over into the room.

4. Settlements were built inside and around a **HILLFORT**.

5. Elites often lived in multistoried roundhouses called **BROCHS**.

6. The tail hairs of **SHETLAND** ponies were used to make fishing lines.

7. Celts loved to drink **BEER**.

The Religion of the Celts before Christianity

What we know for sure is that the Celtic tribes were polytheistic. That means they believed in many gods.

The different Celtic tribes might not have worshiped all the same deities *(gods and goddesses)*. They did have similar belief systems, though. The deities had power over water, air, thunder, rain, harvests, and physical objects, such as a house or a barn. They had power over everything that could influence people's lives.

The ancient Celts believed that everything in nature had a spirit. We call this belief animism. Animals, insects, plants, pebbles, rocks, rivers, lakes, and springs were inhabited by spirits. Trees and groves were seen as holy places. Oak trees were sacred, and the mistletoe that twined around the oak tree was even more holy. Can you imagine how respectfully everything on the earth was treated?

Captivating Celtic Deities

The Morrigan – The Morrigan was the Dagda's consort *(wife)*. She was the goddess of birth, prophecy, fate, and war. In battle, she was a black crow that protected warriors. She also chose who would be killed. The Celts saw her as a guardian of their lands.

Most Celtic gods were shapeshifters. This means they could change their appearance into different humans or animals. The Morrigan, for instance, was a shapeshifting goddess who influenced all the cycles of human life. She could appear as a beautiful young woman, a mother, a scary old woman, or a crow or raven.

The Morrigan was also associated with the banshee, a scary, loud spirit resembling an old woman. People would know that someone would die soon if they saw her appear. She would wail *(cry)*, moan, and even scream into the night.

The Dagda – The Dagda presided over life, death, magic, and wisdom. Depictions of the Dagda show him as a very large man with a magical staff, a harp, and a cauldron. The Dagda had the power to kill people and make them come to life again. His cauldron was bottomless and filled with food, showing his love for eating.

Brigid – Brigid was a red-haired Celtic goddess Brigid. She presided over nature, waterways, rivers, wells, domestic animals, healing, poetry, passion, fire, and metalworking.

Scholars think this goddess was later used by Catholic monks as the inspiration for Saint Brigid. Saint Brigid pleaded with the king of County Kildare in Ireland to give her enough land to build a monastery. He said she could only have as much land as her cloak could cover. Her cloak spread over hundreds of acres when she laid it on the ground.

Brigid.

Lugh – Lugh was the god of the harvest for some Celtic tribes. He was called Lugus by the tribes in Brittany and Lleu Llaw Gyffes in Wales. Ritual sacrifices to him throughout the seasons were believed to ensure crops grew. The people wanted to make sure they had a good harvest.

In other Celtic myths, Lugh was worshiped as the god of the sun and the light. He was also revered as a warrior god.

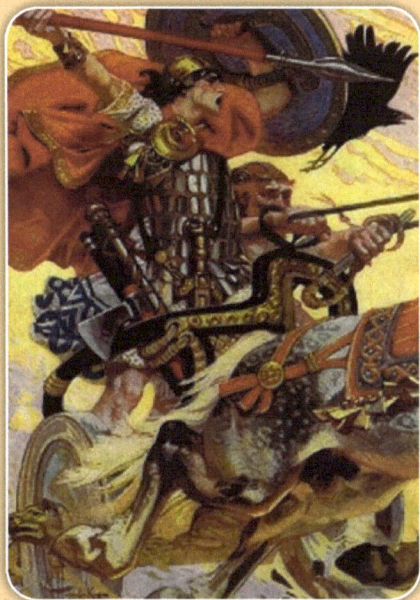

Lugh is believed to have been reincarnated as the Celtic Irish hero Cuchulain, who was Lugh's son.
https://commons.wikimedia.org/wiki/File:Cuinbattle.jpg

Lugh's nickname was "Lugh of the long arm" because of the long spear he carried. He could command this spear to strike an enemy and then return to him.

He was the god of oath-keeping and a judge. He was said to be a brilliant trickster as well.

The Myth of Lir

Lir *(leer)* was a mythical king in Ireland. He and his wife had four beautiful children—three boys and one girl.

His wife died suddenly. Lir married again. His second wife was very jealous when she saw how much King Lir loved his children.

LÉR AND THE SWANS

Lir and his cursed children.
https://commons.wikimedia.org/wiki/File:Ler_swans_Millar.jpg

One sunny afternoon, she took the children to a nearby lake and cast a spell on them. They were turned into four white swans. The spell was to last for nine hundred years before they turned back into humans again.

However, that was not enough punishment. The evil queen made it so that the swans had to live in a different lake every three hundred years.

There are different versions of this story. One version says that the swan children ended up in a lake near a Christian church during their last three hundred years. A friendly monk took care of them. The swans could hear the church bells ring from the lake. They loved the sound of it.

When the nine hundred years were up, they turned back into their human forms. Of course, they were very old and weak. They knew that death was near. Their only wish was to be baptized in the Christian faith before they died. Their wish was granted, and they died in peace.

Festivals

We know that the Celts celebrated many festivals. They loved a good party as much as they loved a good fight. Festivals were held throughout the year to celebrate the changes in seasons.

A modern-day Samhain celebration in Scotland.

Festivals were joyous occasions. People danced around bonfires, ate meat, and drank lots of mead or beer. The wealthy even drank wine imported from France and Italy.

Did you know that modern-day Halloween comes from an old Celtic festival called Samhain? It was the celebration of the end of the harvest and the end of summer. Some scholars call Samhain the "Celtic New Year."

Celtic Mythical Creatures and Spirits

Celtic stories are known for their mythical creatures and their interactions with humans and the environment. It was a way for the Celts to explain how things came to be or why things happened. Here are just a few of those magical creatures.

Fairies – You may be familiar with Tinkerbell from *Peter Pan*. In Celtic mythology, they live in an invisible world that exists with our world. They could be nice, but they would be mean if people did not respect them. People would give fairies gifts to please them.

Leprechauns – Leprechauns are a kind of fairy. They are small men who like to play tricks on humans. Today, we think of leprechauns wearing green, but they originally wore red. We also think they have a pot of gold hidden under the end of a rainbow.

Kelpies – A kelpie is a water spirit that haunts Scottish rivers and lakes. It looked like a horse, but it could shapeshift into a human. Kelpies would entice people to follow them. When they got close to a river or lake, the kelpie would drown the person.

From Pagans to Christians

The Romans brought Christianity to Britain. Catholic monks and bishops set about to convert the pagans. They traveled to Britain and Ireland. However, some of the Celts were set in their ways.

Many Celtic beliefs and rituals remained sacred to the Celts. Some Celts practiced them in secret. The monks used Celtic beliefs to make Christianity more appealing. The Romans also used force to make the Celts convert.

Christian monks and bishops recorded much of the knowledge we have of this period. Saint Columba built a monastic community on the island of Iona, where he was later buried. The island became famous as a place of learning. Many kings were buried there.

Can you unscramble these anagrams to find the names of Celtic deities?

unad

agdad

irl

ganromri

gulh

aints irbdig

From left to right:

Danu

Saint Brigid

Dagda

Lir

Morrigan

Lugh

Much of our knowledge about the Celts comes from art and artifacts excavated by archaeologists. Grave goods are valuable in figuring out what items looked like and what people treasured.

The ancient Celts were expert metalworkers, which gave them a big advantage during the Iron Age. Iron is much stronger than bronze and does not decay like wood. Celts made their plow points, arrow tips, and spearheads from iron. They also used iron to create plaques and sculptures of their gods and warriors.

Iron and iron goods were some of the Celts' most important trade goods. However, they used bronze for most artwork and some everyday utensils.

Celtic gold-plated bronze disc.
Gun Powder Ma, CC BY-SA 3.0 <https://creativecommons.org/licenses/by-sa/3.0>,
via Wikimedia Commons; https://commons.wikimedia.org/w/index.php?curid=9646007

The Coligny Calendar

One of the most interesting Celtic artifacts was discovered near a small town in France in 1897. Scholars long believed it was a type of calendar. The artifact had several metal pieces with holes, pegs, numbers, and letters in Celtic, Greek, and Roman. They called it the Coligny *(ko-lee-nee)* calendar.

It took scholars until 1989 to figure out what kind of calendar it was and how it worked. The original had been mostly destroyed. Only around 45 percent of the pieces were recovered. With the help of computer models, scientists were able to reconstruct most of the missing pieces and work out what the item's purpose.

Broken pieces of the bronze Coligny Calendar are on display in the Galo Roman Museum, Lyon, France.
https://commons.wikimedia.org/w/index.php?curid=194998

It was a lunar-solar calendar that tracked time by using the movements of the sun and the moon. The Celts measured time by moving pegs in the calendar. It ensured that planting, harvesting, and festivals always fell in the right seasons.

Ceremonial Shields

Ordinary Celtic war shields were made of wood and leather with metal buckles. Shields used for ceremonial purposes were often made with decorated sheets of bronze.

A great example of a Celtic ceremonial shield was recovered from the Thames River. It dates to between 350 and 50 BCE. The Battersea Shield can be viewed in the British Museum today. It was crafted from bronze sheet metal and decorated with reliefs and engravings.

The Battersea Shield.
British Museum, CC0, via Wikimedia Commons;
https://commons.wikimedia.org/wiki/File:
British_Museum_Battersea_Shield.jpg

The shield's twenty-seven framed studs were once filled with red glass. Each stud is connected to the others, possibly to show that all elements of life are connected. This shield is presumed to have been thrown into the river as an offering to the gods to ensure the Celts won a battle.

Cauldrons

Cauldrons are magnificent examples of Celtic metal craftsmanship. They symbolized regeneration, abundance, and wealth. A cauldron was viewed as a magical container that would always ensure a never-ending food supply. They were considered a gift from the gods.

These large ornate cooking pots were suspended over a cooking fire with chains. Cauldrons were usually made from bronze sheet metal.

The Gundestrup Cauldron.
Rosemania, CC BY 2.0 <https://creativecommons.org/licenses/by/2.0>,
via Wikimedia Commons; https://commons.wikimedia.org/w/index.php?curid=9404289

The Gundestrup Cauldron from Denmark is handcrafted from gilded silver and dates to approximately the 1st century BCE. Relief panels depict scenes of Celtic gods and myths.

The eight outer panels depict some Celtic gods wearing torcs. The five inner panels include scenes like the sacrifice of a bull, Celtic warriors, griffins *(creatures with the head and wings of an eagle and the body of a lion)*, leopards, and elephants.

Sculptures

Wood and stone were carved and cut into sculptures. Sculptures from bronze and iron were hammered into a shape or cast by pouring hot metal into a mold. These items were engraved or grooved to create a pattern. Enamel, precious stones, coral, shells, and glass were used to decorate sculptures.

Some early Celt artworks survived. Many are now on display in museums. In the Glauberg Museum in Hesse, Germany, for example, is a life-sized sculpture of a warrior dating to the 5th century BCE. The warrior is wearing a tunic, a torc necklace with three pendants, and an elaborate leaf crown. The statue is named "Prince of Glauberg."

The Prince of Glauberg.

Wooden sculptures were usually carved from oak. They often represented warrior gods. These sculptures often had a hooded cloak and sometimes a metal torc. These statues are thought to have stood at Celtic religious sites.

Brooches

Ancient Celts were extremely proud of their brooches. Brooches were originally used to pin clothes together. They eventually became status symbols. Brooches were worn by men, women, and children.

Many brooches and pins were formed in the shape of animals, particularly horses. Snakes, human heads, drums, and bells were also popular. More abstract shapes, like knots and spirals, became fashionable later.

Expensive brooches and pins were made of gold and decorated with precious stones or other materials.

The Tara Brooch.

The penannular *(penan-nu-lar)* brooch was a circle with a pin that could turn and pass through the circle. This left the cloth visible in the open area at the center of the brooch.

The Tara Brooch in the National Museum of Ireland is an example of a penannular brooch. Another famous brooch is the Braganza Brooch on display at the British Museum.

Torcs

A torc was a neckband worn around the necks of Celtic kings, chiefs, distinguished warriors, and the elite. The opening of a torc was worn in the front. Torcs were offered in rituals or buried with their wearer to be used in the afterlife.

The designs of torcs vary. The neckband could be twisted, plain, hollow, or solid. Torcs were made from different intertwined metals, such as gold, silver, and bronze. The ends at the front opening could be shaped like hoops, disks, spheres, or animal heads.

The Snettisham Great Torc is housed in the British Museum. It dates to between 150 and 50 BCE. It was found near the village of Snettisham, Norfolk, England. The craftsman of this beautiful piece used gold alloy *(gold, silver, and copper)* to design

The Snettisham torc.
Johnbod, CC BY-SA 3.0 <https://creativecommons.org/licenses/by-sa/3.0>, via Wikimedia Commons; https://commons.wikimedia.org /wiki/File:Snettisham_HoardDSCF6580.jpg

this torc. It has sixty-four strands of gold alloy twisted into eight ropes. Each rope has eight strands. The ends, also called terminals, were cast using molds and then welded onto the ropes.

Chapter 6 Activity

Can you find the words from the word bank?

C	W	O	O	D	X	B	R	O	N	Z	E
Z	E	P	G	R	E	G	O	R	I	A	N
L	B	L	A	Q	T	O	Y	F	Q	G	D
P	L	A	T	S	Z	K	M	J	P	S	L
R	O	N	C	I	X	T	Q	A	L	U	E
U	C	T	D	A	C	O	L	I	G	N	Y
D	H	U	V	N	I	C	W	E	L	H	F
C	D	T	X	I	R	L	R	O	M	A	N
V	E	R	W	M	O	O	U	O	I	B	L
J	U	L	I	A	N	B	D	E	S	K	U
W	P	K	M	L	B	T	Z	X	O	S	C

Word Bank:

CELTIC	SUN	PLANT
COLIGNY (calendar)	IRON	ANIMAL
WOOD	BRONZE	

C	W	O	O	D	X	B	R	O	N	Z	E
Z	E	P	G	R	E	G	O	R	I	A	N
L	B	L	A	Q	T	O	Y	F	Q	G	D
P	L	A	T	S	Z	K	M	J	P	S	L
R	O	N	C	I	X	T	Q	A	L	U	E
U	C	T	D	A	C	O	L	I	G	N	Y
D	H	U	V	N	I	C	W	E	L	H	F
C	D	T	X	I	R	L	R	O	M	A	N
V	E	R	W	M	O	O	U	O	I	B	L
J	U	L	I	A	N	B	D	E	S	K	U
W	P	K	M	L	B	T	Z	X	O	S	C

**Are you wide awake? PROVE IT by finding any other English words or names in this puzzle! **

According to ancient Greek and Roman writers, the Celts were bloodthirsty, ferocious warriors. Their enemies did not know that it was mostly acting. The Celts used their appearance as a battle tactic to scare their enemies. It often worked!

Facing an army of Celts must have been terrifying for any attacker. Just picture the scene when the Romans invaded.

On one side of the battlefield are troops of disciplined Roman soldiers. They march in perfect formation into battle to meet their enemy.

A short distance away is a horde of tall, muscular Celts. They shout and scream. They are eager for the fight. The Celts are on horseback and on foot. Some ride in chariots.

Some of the Celts are naked. Their bodies are painted or tattooed. Others wear an assortment of clothing, including leather body armor and metal or leather helmets. Their long hair is coated in white lime wash *(a mixture of limestone and water)*. This makes their hair white and stiff. They messed their hair up on purpose to appear scarier.

The Celts charge like a pack of hungry, wild dogs. Screams fill the air. Their iron weapons glint in the sunlight as they swing them. The Celt horse riders plunge into the Roman front lines, their long, sharp swords slicing left and right. To tell you the truth, I think I might have turned and run if I was facing them!

Weapons

The Celts were expert ironsmiths. They mainly used swords in battles. They also used axes, knives, spears, and lances. Some of these weapons had serrated *(jagged)* edges.

The Celts also used bows and arrows. They used leather slingshots to hurl stones and clay missiles.

Celtic sword and scabbard circa 60 BCE.
PHGCOM, CC BY-SA 3.0 <https://creativecommons.org/licenses/by-sa/3.0>,
via Wikimedia Commons; https://commons.wikimedia.org/wiki/File:Celtic_sword_and_scabbard_circa_60_BCE.jpg

Warriors of high status and those on horseback carried swords with long, straight blades. These swords could be up to thirty-five inches (eighty-nine centimeters) long.

Swords and knives were sheathed in wooden or leather scabbards that hung from their waists. Scabbards and swords were often decorated with gold, silver, ivory, or precious stones.

Armor, Shields, and Helmets

Warriors of high status often wore breastplates, chainmail, leather, or some kind of hard material. Stags, horses, bulls, and boars were depicted on body armor and shields.

Shields were oval-shaped and large. They shielded most of the body. They were made from wood and leather. Celts made shields out of metal, but those were usually used for ceremonial purposes.

Some Celtic warriors wore bronze, iron, or leather helmets decorated with horns or feathers.

A Celtic parade helmet.
Xuan Che; https://creativecommons.org/licenses/by/2.0/.
https://www.flickr.com/photos/69275268@N00/4121249212

Battles with Rome

The Celts and Romans fought many battles even before the Celts migrated to Britain. Historians recount the tale of a fierce Celtic chief named Brennus. He sacked the city of Rome in 390 BCE.

A painting of Boudica.
https://commons.wikimedia.org/wiki/File:Queen_Boudica_by_John_Opie.jpg

The Celts often lost against the Romans. The Roman armies were stronger. They burned villages and destroyed crops. Some Celts were enslaved. Some were forced into the Roman armies. Villages were forced to pay tribute *(money or goods)* to Rome at times.

After Rome invaded Britain in 43 CE, conflicts broke out. The Celts would seek peace, but the battles with the Romans would eventually begin again.

The most successful and famous Celtic revolt against the Romans in Britain was led by Queen Boudica of the Iceni tribe. Although they burned Roman cities and won several battles, they were defeated in the end.

Chapter 7 Activity

Which statements below are true, and which are false? Remember, you may go back through the chapter to find the answers!

	Question	True	False
1.	The Celts used scare tactics to frighten their enemies.		
2.	Celtic warriors were cowards.		
3.	Celtic spear points and knives were made of iron.		
4.	Roman soldiers were trained and disciplined.		
5.	Celtic warriors fought to protect their lands and possessions.		
6.	Celts were led by generals chosen from the Druids.		
7.	Celtic warriors were never treated like heroes.		
8.	Celtic warriors fought in the nude because they wanted their clothes to stay clean.		

Chapter 7 Answers

	Question	True	False
1.	The Celts used scare tactics to frighten their enemies.	✗	
2.	Celtic warriors were cowards.		✗
3.	Celtic spear points and knives were made of iron.	✗	
4.	Roman soldiers were trained and disciplined.	✗	
5.	Celtic warriors fought to protect their lands and possessions.	✗	
6.	Celts were led by generals chosen from the Druids.		✗
7.	Celtic warriors were never treated like heroes.		✗
8.	Celtic warriors fought in the nude because they wanted their clothes to stay clean.		✗

There is a difference between symbols, crests, and logos. You may have heard people talk about brand names when buying clothes or products. The name of a company is often associated with a specific image. That image may be a picture or the way the company's name is written. Coca-Cola is a good example.

Sometimes, symbols represent belief systems, like the Celtic trinity knot or the colors or patterns on a country's flag.

Illustration of the Celtic trinity knot.
Madboy74, CC BY-SA 4.0 <https://creativecommons.org/licenses/by-sa/4.0>,
via Wikimedia Commons; https://commons.wikimedia.org/wiki/File:Coa_Illustration_Cross_Triquetra.svg

Well-known Celtic symbols are mostly from Ireland and Scotland. However, they are sold and worn as jewelry all over the world. There are so many symbols that we can only mention a few of them here.

Shamrock

The shamrock is a small clover plant with three leaves on every stem. It is the national plant and a symbol of Ireland. The story goes that Saint Patrick, the patron saint of Ireland, used the shamrock to explain the concept of the Christian Trinity. However, there are so many folk tales involving Saint Patrick that we may never be sure which ones are true.

If you find a four-leaf clover, you are said to have good luck. Have you ever found a four-leaf clover before?

Harp

The harp is one of Ireland's national symbols. In the days of the Celts, bards often played music on a harp as they told their stories. When Ireland became a kingdom, a harp was added to the national flag.

A harp made in the Celtic style. This harp is from the 1950s.

Claddagh Ring

The clasped hands of this popular ring supposedly date back about two thousand years. The ring is made in the shape of two hands clasping a heart with a crown on it. The heart means love, the crown means loyalty, and the clasped hands mean friendship. The ring can be given as a token of lasting friendship or romantic love.

Claddagh ring.
I, Royalcladdagh, CC BY-SA 3.0 <http://creativecommons.org/licenses/by- sa/3.0/>,
via Wikimedia Commons; https://commons.wikimedia.org/wiki/File:Claddaghring.jpg

The Celtic Knot

This symbol comes in many shapes and sizes. It can have pointed or straight corners.

The Celtic knot is used in so many different ways that it would take a whole book to describe them all. The three strands of the original Celtic knot represented fire, water, and earth. It is made in a looped design with no visible beginning or end.

An example of a Celtic knot.

Celtic Cross

Celtic crosses predate Christianity. They are a good example of how pagan symbolism was used by Christians to convert the Celts.

The ancient pagan Celts believed the circle in the Celtic cross stood for the sun. For Christians, the cross symbolizes the cross Jesus died on.

An example of a Celtic cross.

Unscramble the letters of each word to find a Celtic symbol.

SCRAMBLED LETTERS	CLUE	ANSWER
1. RSKOCHMA	A small, green leafy plant	
2. RHPA	A musical instrument on Ireland's flag	
3. TKON EITCLC	It has many shapes and forms. It has no visible beginning or end.	
4. TCILEC SORCS	It replaced a pagan symbol of a similar shape.	
5. DCALDCHA INRG	It symbolizes love, loyalty, and friendship	

1. SHAMROCK

2. HARP

3. CELTIC KNOT

4. CELTIC CROSS

5. CLADDACH RING

The Celts remained separated into many tribes all over Britain and Ireland for centuries. Each had their own chieftain. Later, they had kings. In Ireland, there was a high king over all the other Irish kingdoms.

Tribes fought against each other. They also married each other and feasted together. They were both friends and enemies. Sometimes, larger tribes took over smaller tribes.

And then came the Romans.

The Romans

During the Gallic Wars, the Romans defeated the Gauls. (Do you remember them? They were the Celts who lived in mainland Europe). After the Gallic Wars, a famous Roman leader named Julius Caesar tried to invade Britain twice. He did so in 55 and 54 BCE, but he was not successful.

The Romans invaded Britain again in 43 CE. This time, the Romans were successful. They took over Britain. The Romans named their new territory the province of Britannia. The conquest took a little over forty years.

Roman soldiers built forts, roads, bridges, garrisons, and cities in Britannia. They gave them Latin names.

Some Celtic tribes were never conquered. Other tribes revolted. The Roman culture was adopted in a few conquered areas, mostly in the east of England.

Britain supplied Rome with grain and meat. The Romans also used the Celts' excellent metalworking skills to make superior weapons and jewelry.

Roman Conquest of Britain
43 – 84

Based on Frere's *Britannia*,
Jones & Mattingly's *Atlas
of Roman Britain*, and
The Agricola by Tacitus

0　　　km　　100
0　　ml　　50

Campaigns
- 43 (Claudius)
- 43-47 (Aulus Plautius)
- 47-52 (Ostorius Scapula)
- 52-57 (Didius Gallus)
- 57 (Quintus Veranus)
- 58-60 (Suetonius Paulinus)
- 69-71 (Vettius Bolanus)
- 71-73 (Pettilius Cerialis)
- 73-77 (Julius Frontinus)
- 77-84 (Agricola)

A look at how the Romans slowly took over Britain.

Time marched on. The mighty Roman Empire, like all empires, went into decline. Troops were withdrawn from Britain to defend Rome. Britain had been a province of Rome for nearly four hundred years, but the Romans never conquered all of it.

The Anglo-Saxons

After the Roman troops left Britain in 410 CE, others saw a chance to invade. The invaders were the Angles, Saxons, Jutes, and Frisians. We call them the Anglo-Saxons today.

The Anglo-Saxons were Germanic farmers and warriors who spoke Indo-European languages. Their homelands were around the areas of today's Denmark, Germany, and the Netherlands.

Their warriors were hired as soldiers by a king in England to drive out raiders from the north, mainly the Picts and Scottish Celts. The Anglo-Saxon warriors realized that England's rich farmland was better than their lands. They decided to take it over.

Many Anglo-Saxons did not want to live in Roman stone buildings. They wanted the same type of houses they had in their homelands. They built one-roomed huts with thatched roofs. The chief's house was the largest. It had space for an extended family, warriors, and servants.

The villages were surrounded by high wooden fences to keep wild animals and enemies out. Sometimes, the farm animals were kept in the village.

Some of the chiefs realized the stone walls of the Roman cities provided greater protection, so they moved there.

The Anglo-Saxons were pagans. They likely had as many gods as the Celts. They built wooden temples for their gods. These temples were later converted into churches after the pope in Rome sent a monk to convert them to Christianity.

This monk was Saint Augustine. He arrived in England in 597 CE. Augustine convinced the Anglo-Saxon king of Kent, Ethelbert, to become a Christian. Other tribes followed. England soon became a Christian country.

A Fountain of Tales and Legends

The Anglo-Saxons and the Celts fought many battles. The Celts wanted to protect and defend their lands. We don't have a lot of information about this period. Records from this period were recorded by monks and abbots after Christianity became popular. They mostly recorded stories that would help them promote Christianity and point out the folly *(foolishness)* of paganism.

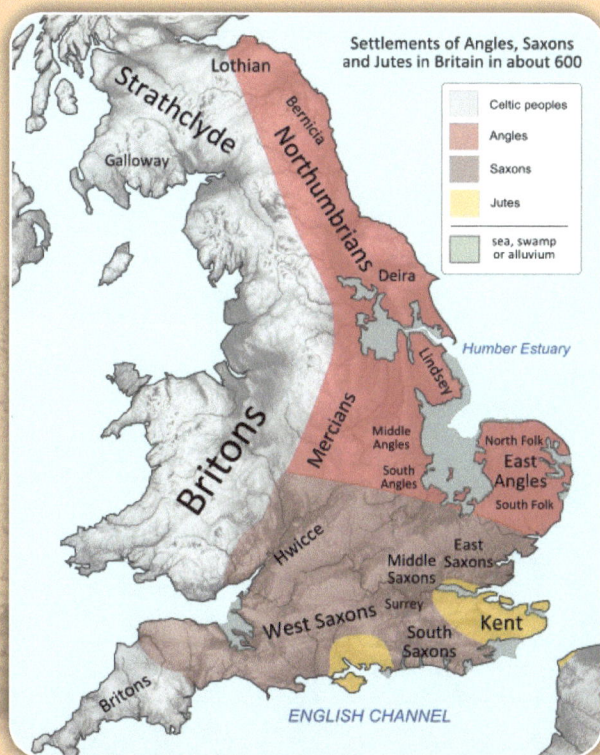

What Britain looked like in 600 CE.

After the Romans left, Celts created new kingdoms in England based on Celtic traditions. Many new kingdoms were also formed by powerful Anglo-Saxon leaders. The Celts chose their rulers. The Anglo-Saxon kingship was hereditary. Their rulers and leaders had more privileges than the working classes.

The Celts never truly disappeared. Their traditions were no longer celebrated as they had in the past. However, the Celts married other people groups. Some left Britain. Today, over one hundred million people are related to the ancient Celts.

Can you complete and color in this picture to look like a Celtic warrior?

If you want to learn more about tons of other exciting
historical periods, check out our other books!

BILLY WELLMAN

EGYPTIAN MYTHOLOGY
FOR KIDS

Enthralling Myths and Legends of
Gods, Goddesses, and Mythological Creatures

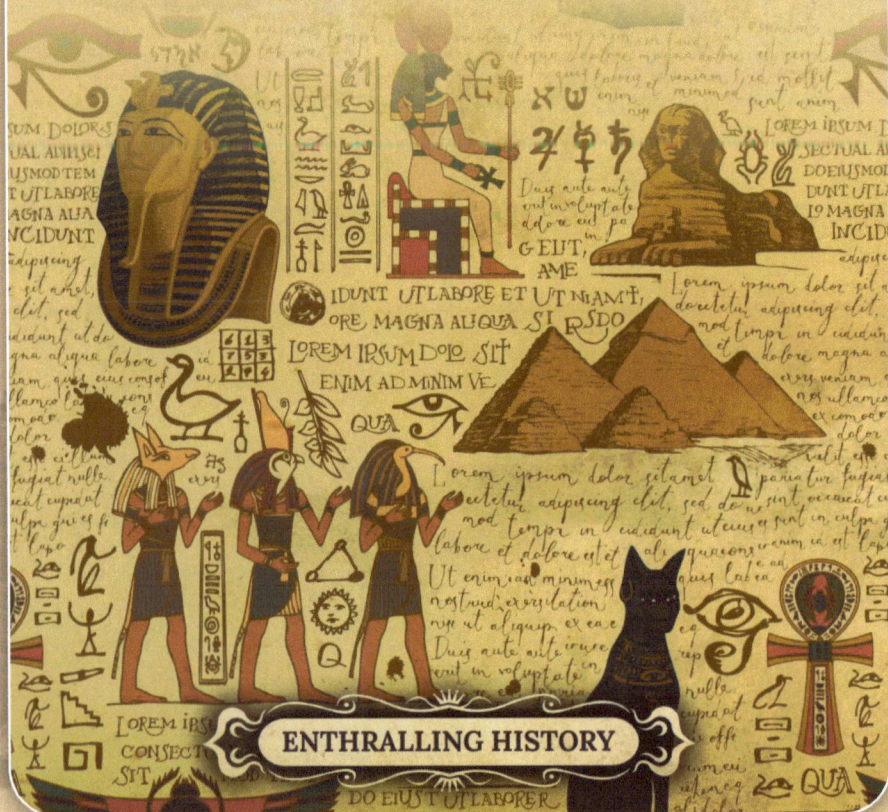

ENTHRALLING HISTORY

SUGGESTED READING

Books:

Deary, Terry. *Cut-throat Celts (Horrible Histories)*. 2022.

Green, Jen. *National Geographic Investigates: Ancient Celts: Archaeology Unlocks the Secrets of the Celts' Past*. 2008.

Pinard, Chris. *Celtic Mythology for Kids: Tales of Selkies, Giants, and the Sea*. 2020.

Amazon.com: The Celts: Search for a Civilization eBook: Roberts, Alice: Kindle Store

Websites:

https://kids.britannica.com/kids/article/Celt/352934

https://celts.mrdonn.org/

https://localhistories.org/celtic-daily-life/

VIDEOS:

"A Day in the Life of a Celt." https://youtu.be/nthEmXpT7ww.

"Iron Age Diaries: Day One." https://youtu.be/qQJ7zFDYvDo. Check out the other videos in this series!

"The Rise of the Celts in Central Europe." https://youtu.be/M-sRb-tNlKI.

www.ingramcontent.com/pod-product-compliance
Lightning Source LLC
Chambersburg PA
CBHW042127080426
42734CB00005B/77